CROSS GUARD
CHRONICLES

THE DIARY CONTINUES...

I0095900

Carolina Ayala-Velasquez

Carolina M-G Ayala

Alameda, CA

Carolina Ayala-Velasquez

Ordering Information:
Amazon. Or, reach out through Instagram "crossguardchronicles"

Cross Guard Chronicles/ Carolina Ayala-Velasquez. — 1st ed.
ISBN 979-8-9855006-5-3

ALL NAMES USED IN THIS BOOK ARE MADE
UP AND NOT NAMES OF THE ACTUAL PEOPLE
I HAVE MET.

MY EXPERIENCE IS ONLY MINE, I AM NOT
AND CANNOT SPEAK FOR ALL CROSSING-
GUARDS OR PEOPLE.

MY DIARY IS MINE. MY EXPERIENCES AND
JOURNEY THAT I AM CHOOSING TO SHARE.
LESSONS LEARNED, FEARS, GRATITUDES
AND SO MUCH MORE.

SOME RANDOM THOUGHTS, SOME
INCOMPLETE. SOME FULLY WRITTEN OUT,
AND ALL IS OK WITH ME. BECAUSE, THIS IS
MY DIARY.
IMPERFECTLY PERFECT, IT'S REAL AND IT'S
UNIQUE.
IN A WORLD FULL OF "AI"-
HERE IN THE ERRORS AND IMPERFECTIONS
IS WHAT I LIKE.

This book is dedicated to all who I have had the honor of crossing paths with during my time at Stargell and Mosley. Thank you for inspiring me, joining me in community/fun and purpose. Thank you for giving my days a sense of safety, happiness and meaning beyond the job title.

Thank you to my family. For being on the phone with me sometimes when I felt unsafe, for helping me with chalk work when I wanted more hands and ideas, for choosing your own paths in which helped me choose this new one for myself.

Why do you cross guard?
Crossguard is one position I wasn't searching for. Not specifically. I was looking to get back out into the world, literally- to get out of the house. I was working from home home and doing so much from home, I was ready to get out for a bit. I knew I didn't want to be indoors in a mask all day. I wanted a part time job, flexibility and income.
When I came across the job description it sounded perfect at the time. The price was "right", for a few hours a day.
It wasn't teaching but maybe it could be in a way. Quickly, my mind was calculating the possible income I could make. It sounded like something that could financially work for us. At that time of applying, all of my kids were schooling from home and we had family and sitters readily avaiable.
I thought of the other benefits that could come from this job, such as: new experience, exercise depending on the distance and location while knowing it would be local, facing fears and anxities of getting out of the house in this way while still in a pandemic and so much more.

Why do I continue to do this work?
I have definitley had some situations that made me question "is it worth it?"
I continue to show up because I love the community I serve. I think about that location and how a crossguard is needed and how the community appreciates me. I know they would appreciate any crossguard there but I have made connections. I have created something

more here. I continue to do this work because I still love the hours and pay. I still love the exercise I get, so much that I have requested- several times to not be re-located.

I like who I am , while in this work. I like how I show up. I like having another purpose that drives me and fuels me and feels rewarding in several ways.

This does not mean I don't have complaints. It does not mean that everything is great or good all the time. It doesn't mean I don't wish some things were different. It doesn't even mean that the money always feels worth it.

It does mean, that right now- it all, still feels worth it to me.

Why do you chalk work?

It started off as an idea in the 2021-2022 school year, when I started cross guard work in February of 2022. The idea came from me wanting to build connections and community outside of the barriers of masks and pandemic rules and fears and lifestyles.

I also started doing the chalk work because sometimes people would say things or try to start conversation in the middle of the street and I would feel disrespectful to not be able to engage in the a full way. So , I figured, one way to show I was listening and wanting to respond could be through chalk. It continues to inspire, motivate and teach me.

My intentions can shift when I am writing or drawing: sometimes to create opportunity for movement or reading or math, engage families in conversations or play and invite fun. Those are just a few examples of some intentions. I don't believe every message will serve every person who comes across it. But if even one person is served in any way, even if that one person is just me- it's enough.

Social media allows this work to go beyond this physical space. You can follow some of these adventures on crossguardchronicles (Instagram.)

The first Day of School

I have been anticipating this time, the first day of school.

This year, for my home and family- we have 3 of our children starting school again, here in Alameda. Two of our kids have been online/remote learning for the past couple of years.

I debated on taking the morning shift off, at least- to be able to be with my kids as they transition.

I ultimately decided I would work, not only because we "need" the income but because I thought it would be better for me to be busy with work and helping other families transition on their first day and that my husband deserved this time to be with our kids and support them. It was a lot of letting go of the need to control and know things.

As far as work, I had anxiety about "what if I forgot everything I learned because I had summer off." Anxiety about having to deal with cars and people in a rush because of the first day and because of not having a crossing guard around during the summer. All of the thoughts of having to re-teach the community during these two hours of time when it comes to:

waiting for me to give a verbal ok to cross, walking bikes and scooters, looking both ways even when a crossing guard is present, so many things.

Then I thought about it more, we are always teaching these things. Whether summer or winter break or everyday life.
New families and people in the community come at random times. The teaching is on-going. The learning is on-going as well, for me and them.

It's always the nights I need to get the most and best sleep, that's the most challenging 🧕
Even when I'm exhausted😫😩
Prayers for my children, our children, ourselves.
Praying that teachers, strudents, families and communities feel supported. I pray that they are. That rescources are shared and made aware.
I pray for the counselors, siblings, caretakers, crossing guards and all who play a part in the village we depend on.
Praying that the news and social media, both past and present can give us all space to breathe and be.
I pray for everyone's health, safety and happiness

Summer doesn't have to end just because school begins.

8/12/22

The ideas are flooding my mind already, about what I might write when it comes to chalk work.

Welcome back.

How are you feeling?

What did you love about summer?

Which grade level has been your favorite? Why? (adults feel free to answer as well. Think back.)

If you could choose your school lunch, what would you be eating today?

*I could love you even forever. doesn't mean we'd be together... Lol, yes diary. Sometimes other thoughts just come to mind. I am human and have other layers beyond this job position. But, back to the topic...

"I wish these cars would slow down. Morning one back to work is done."

8/15/22

It's a Monday and middle of the month. It's back to school day for Ruby Bridges and for my kids at "Alameda High" and "Wood Middle school." Some schools near Ruby Bridges already started last week!

Woah, hello tummy emotions. You've really ramped up by 6am 😓🙏⏰
My oldest daughter was up and I'm not sure she actually slept. We both were the last ones up last night and first ones awake this morning.

I am glad to have had a few moments with her before I left.

I even woke up our oldest son on my way out.

My two youngest were still sleeping as I went out the door.

This is the first time ever it feels like that I won't be present for the first day of school.

Instead I will be cross guarding for other children and families on their first days.

I had plans to write each of my kids a letter, since I wouldn't be home in the morning but ended up sending texts.

I started my sons lunch but didn't finish.

Nervous for work, knowing we have to get the cars, community and families back into routine of having a cross guard present again.

Thankful for my bike ride to sit with these feelings and thoughts, while getting fresh air and drinking water.

As I am crossing kids, I feel my emotions creep in. The thoughts and guilt and feelings, of leaving my kids and being here instead of there.

I should be walking my kids to school today, making them breakfast, taking their first day pictures.

I chose to work, to keep my brain and heart busy. To give my husband the opportunity and time. To give the kids their space. To trust on the people, I can lean on.

I am so thankful this morning that it was light out for my bike ride. I don't know if it was warm out or if it was just the bike ride and emotions but I was hot. By my morning shift, ride home- I was drenched in sweat and had to change everything.

Thank you bike ride. Thank you sweat. Thank you, water- even though I chugged you instead of enjoying you.

Thank you chalk, time and thoughts for helping me create some fun for this beautiful first day.

I am so thankful my husband took today off. To be present for our kids and me.

I am so thankful for headbands I invested in yesterday. Because I love the way they fit.

I am thankful for the returning families and community members who welcomed me back, asked about my summer and said they were happy to see me. For the hand waves. The people who stopped to play hopscotch or engage in conversation over written words, some even took photos.

I could look at all of this so different. But leaning into gratitude is what brings me peace and happiness.

"I loved it before I knew how much more there would be to love."

8/16/22

I am thankful for a morning bike ride and for the first day of school being yesterday.

"From sunburns yesterday to rain drops this morning."

8/17/22

I am reminding myself that we live in a world where people cross the street.

Maybe that sounds like "duh" or even makes you laugh. But I came to this thought when feeling emotions of what others may be thinking or feeling. Sometimes I can feel judged by drivers or even people walking. I came across this thought, we live in a world where people cross streets, and I am just doing my job. I am helping families feel safer, cars be more considerate and I am just doing a job that would get done with or without me.

That realization feels good to have and hold.

To help me get out of my head.

How will we hold on to summer and create a life we love?

I am already thinking of my next book,part 2 of this journey, the ideas that come to mind:

I can use chalk work as questions, to journal in a book. I can use pictures to separate pages or add as a gallery.

"I thought that was only for the kids" a father says about me crossing just him.

8/18/22

A guy running saw me writing and said "I love that."
This job is so scary. To be safe, to keep others safe.

"You don't have to keep pedaling. You can stop and still move forward, in rest."

8/19/22

Cam asks me if I have worked this site always. She continues to say I am very brave to do this work.

This week I learned...
This week I was reminded...
This week I was inspired by...
This week I am celebrating...
This week I will do _____Differently.

8/22/22
What is something fun you did over the weekend?

What is an anchor thought you will use to help ground you this week? Or just today?

A little girl asked me "how are you feeling?" I jumped on happy and said "I am feeling happy". She said "me too."
Whether I did or didn't feel that way prior to her asking, doesn't matter. Because, in that moment I am happy.

A high-schooler who had no words all last week, today said "you too" when I said good-morning and hope you have a good day.
We can't predict or assume. "why should I even try" was a thought but I am so happy I kept being me.

I saw a young girl hug a tree across the street. It made me think of "have you ever hugged a tree?" as something to write with chalk. But that question will get you a yes or no answer. Then I thought "what does hugging a tree feel like? Why would someone hug a tree?" that can get someone to try it or elebaortae on their answer, should they choose to read it or participate.

As I was crossing people, I noticed I run out of the street when they are done crossing and I am on my way back to the sidewalk. I asked myself why do I do this. Why do I run out of the street after crossing people, instead of just walk.
My answer: To get out of cars way, to show I am wanting to be out of their way.
I decided then and there to tell myself a new story, that I do not have to rush- because I am not in a rush. I do want to be courtious. I also want to be safe. I want to be respectful and I want to preserve my energy.
I can walk, instead of run.

I am remembering last school year in February when I first started and how the first couple of days I was really fatigued and realized why heat stroke is real and dangerous.
I am remembering how I spent time last school year talking with people from the city to improve the streets. Several days people took pictures of me, asked questions.
I am wondering if it helped at all? This street is so dangerous.

8/23/22

I saw a guy running, he slows down as I enter the street and says "oh, I can take my time now, thank you."

One guy I thought was a high-schooler last year, I found out is actually a parent.

At one point, I saw that the sprinklers might come on where my bike was parked, I didn't move it. Thinking of how hot it is outside and how it can dry and how a free bike wash could be nice. I left it. It did get wet. People crossing were concerned for me, I shared "yay free bike wash and at least its hot out to cool me off and dry my bike."

So many said that was a great way to look at the situation, made people laugh and smile.

Today a mom I have connected with last school year was walking her two boys and she asked my name. She says "I hope I remember." She shares their 3 names after I ask.

8/24/22
Today a family told me "this place needs you."

A little girl asks her parent "why does she run out of the street?" I said how funny, I was asking myself that the other day.

Isn't it crazy to know our thoughts are not just ours. It's all about sharing them.

A girl asks her mom, what is labor day? Wondering why this weekend is a 4day holiday break.
So of course, I write in chalk the googled definition I found.
Questions and research is so important. We can all learn together and because of each other.

Today I walked with a collegeue , thankful her bad times aren't mine.

My site supervisor checked on me today. He mentioned we get a rain jacket after we have been here for 1 year. I am excited for that day to come. Someone quit at paden school so he is looking for more cross guards but isn't here to ask me or move me, just inform me. I know he wanted to move me but I respectfully declined. I also let him know I needed a new stop sign, so- he gave me one. I am thankful for him as a supervisor.

8/25/22
Today a highschooler saw me writing with chalk when I was off work. He said "I never knew it was you doing all this, that's pretty awesome."

Out of a group of 6, 1 child played hopscotch.
I do it for that 1.
I see a mom let her son out of his stroller to play hopscotch because he asked.
What if more parents did this, had the time- to listen, to respond with a yes, to allow the distraction and fun.

A small boy who is not yet in school see's a jeep , a real jeep and is telling his mom "that's mine"
I said to her "its never too early to vision." She says I suppose you are right.
We both had a good laugh and smiles all around.

This morning a young boy was at the feelings drawing and his mom asks "how are you feeling?" he chose "hungry" she says "why, did you not eat your breakfast?" They started walking away in conversation. I am so happy these chalk creations help people talk about their feelings and have conversations.

A guy driving in a car, said "I appreciate you" after waiting while I crossed people.
How wonderful to have people in the community appreciate what you do, especially in my position (you never know if a waiting car is annoyed or not.) Happy this car was not annoyed, but appreciative.

An hour to you may feel like 5 to someone else.

8/26/22
A woman asks "If you are in the street can I turn?"
I cannot tell drivers how to drive or what to do. My job is not to direct traffic, only to stop it. Unfortunatley , whether we have become friends or not- I have to watch how I respond.

As I am riding my bike to my site, a collegue says "just an hour to go"

Here goes my mind again, over-analyzing and wandering off in thoughts.
An hour to you may be 5 hours to another.
(when I think of the work I have waiting for me at home.)
You may get to go home and rest after, someone else may not. It reminded me of when I say similar comments to people.

8/29/22

On my ride home this morning, I saw my site supervisor and a collegue talking, then they said hi and invited me over- so I went.
It felt like a crossguard meet up
He said "I need a whole new roster." Someone didn't show up.
My supervisor is talking about doing a bike safety month. I would love this because it is something that needs to be talked about, especially when it's a concern. It feels good to have a supervisor that cares.

Today two trucks came to work on a pipe across from me. Car conjestion for sure, but at least people have to stop and pay attention. The guys working were funny. I felt safer with them there working, like I have whitnesses if anything happens. Highlight of my day.

A guy on bike saw me riding and said "want to race?" no thank you.

I am learning many things with this job. Like, when you ride your bike in the street , even in the crosswalk- you are considered a motor vehicle. If you want me to cross you, you have to walk it. If you choose to ride, do so outside of the crosswalk. You can run people over and it could create accidents. Thank you crossguard conversations for teaching me more.

The other message I got is "you are here for an hour, it is your job to make it as safe as possible. Best you can."

An elder woman stopped to thank me for keeping everyone safe. " Im from Ohio, I don't live here. So I rely on everyone else to help take care of those I love and with the new baby they're out numbered." she shared. I feel happy to be a part of their story and her appreciation.

I wrote a tornado joke earlier and then the thought came to me that a lot of this community moves and travels and that joke could be not funny. I hope to not trigger or offend anyone. Maybe I am thinking too much. But I can't not now.

8/30/22
Diary gives me permission for imperfection. To just be me, be real.

I got a text this morning on my way to work, one of my kids "feels sick" I have no time to check in. I am wondering if they stay then will we need a doctors note or proof. Do I send them to just be sent home because then its on the school not me. Why do I have to send

my kid just to get sent home knowing I can't pick them up. If my kid comes home then I need a sitter.
I should feel comfortable and powerful enough to keep my child home. Without constant covid tests or doctor appointments or anything, if I feel it's in their best interest.

Now my mind is on the many transitions of back to in-person schooling.
So many transitions: big heavy backpacks, lots more exercise, worse eating...Regular emotions, rules, judgement, masks, fears.

 Adult check in: I'm hungry. She says when she gets to the feelings chalk check in.
I love when adults participate. Whether it's to get the kids inspired or just to be a part of the human experience, it's what it's meant for.

8/31/22
This job is scary.
A go pro on the job would be nice to show how dangerous it can be. I can't take pictures because this is a fast pace job when it's in action.
I can't take pictures of speeding cars, while doing my job.

A few cars stop , wait and thank me.

Labor day is coming, what will you do this 4 day weekend?

9/1/22
A lady walking asks me "when I am driving and you are in the street stopping cars on that side, can I turn on this side?" I let her know I can not direct traffic or tell anyone how to drive. When I am in the street I am stopping all traffic and crossing who needs to and people/cars can come from all angles. She says "I will just stay at a stop if you are in the street" I say thank you.

9/2/22
No work this beautiful Friday, no pay, no school.

"could be worse" translates to gratitude for me.
What could be worse=what could be better.
And leads to ,What already is.

*Don't let anyone tell you what my death should mean or be or bring to you to one day. Let it be what it is. This is the way I grieve, the way I heal. *

Hey diary, yes- all these different thoughts come to me. It would be a crossguard day if it wasn't a day off.

9/5/22
No work this beautiful hot record breaking heat day
I wish my thoughts didn't rush to the fact that a day off means I do not get paid. I do wish we got paid on days off, that would be nice for us.
I will be thankful, thankful I am not working or biking in this heat.

9/6/22
I know that just me riding my bike spreading smiles and "good-mornings" matter

Some kids ride bikes with their parents and the kids will walk their bikes while the parents dont.
I thank them, in front of them. My intention to let the children know I appreciate them and encourage them to continue. My hope that the adults will follow.
I know, as an adult- how frustrating it can be to get off the bike to walk it. I get it.

Today I am feeling like, I could lay down and give up, it's so hot. I don't want to ride back home. I want to wait for shade. I feel my emotions and metal capacity going down.
I can be in my misery or get up and go. Change my mindset.
 I try to talk to myself in more positive ways. I see some people running and working out in this heat and start to realize I can think differently.
And so I did.

9/7/22
What happens if you chase the wind? Can you catch it?
The vest, hat and stop sign do not make me feel safe enough.
This morning a young girl blew kisses to me and said "have a beautiful day"
Cars pretending not to see me, to speed by feeling justified.

I saw some of my family drive by me. It's always nice to see people we care about.

As I watch kids of all ages and sizes pass me by, I am realizing small children carrying big backpacks and how we are taught so early to carry so much. Heavy or not.

A woman says "it's a murder scene out here." I guess because of the busy roads and people and the dangers on the roads.

Someone asks me how I am . I say "it's moment to moment out here."

A parent crossing exchanges words with a driver. The driver was upset he had to come to a complete stop because the woman was scared to cross until he did. He says "why aren't you going" she said "I wasn't sure if you were going to stop, you were going so fast" he says "speed has nothing to do with it." And then, speeds past her before she even makes it to the other side.

9/8/22

This job is so scary. (How many times have I said that? How many times will I feel this?)

I think about this heatwave and how if I was teaching what would I do today?

Lead meditation or yoga, sit in the shade and journal. Talk about the importance of water.

How would I teach today?

Hoping my kids are ok.

This is my book, my diary.

But when it's a book- you change your "diary" pages to "please" others. When it is a book for the public and not just you, is it a true diary?
This time I will go deeper and be even more real. While also having to not be as real, such as I do need to change names and things just to be respectful and safe and it's true, I guess I can't be as real as I would love to be.

9/9/22
Pay day.
Writing with chalk is not a conern, priority or interest to me today. Although I am here early. I am going to sit in the shade and just chill. It's so hot.

I was on the curb showing my sign wanting to cross people. A guy was driving . He gets close enough to show he isn't slowing down and says "oh cmon wait till theyre closer" throwing up his arms yelling out the window with anger in his voice.
I want to say so much.
"you sir, were going too fast in a 25 zone. Although maybe you reached it or close to it when you decided to make comments- you slowed down for that but not enough to stop or to be considerate of the families needing to cross. "
you didn't fully stop, I have no time in-between your speeding and my job description to share any words. Maybe though then this wouldn't have happened. Maybe you should learn patience. Maybe you should come do my job. Maybe leave next time with less rush in your driving to get to where you are going.

I have to attempt to stop traffic, people like you.
Speeding cars, fog, rain, high sun---kids who cross
with or without adults. I have a job to do. I have to stop
cars and people from multiple angles. In hopes for
safety, while risking me and others and comments like
yours.
I feel fine with my choice.

Today I am thankful its not hot enough out to want to
pour water in my hat like yesterday.

9/12/22
Monday.
A woman who saw me doing chalk said "I didn't know
you were the one doing that. It's so awesome, I know
my kids love it."
Another mom "are you the one that does these? They
are so freaking awesome. Really, they make our day"
I got emotional.
Cam's daughter says "wait are you the one who draws
all of these?"
her son says "which one did you do?"
Cam "our other crossing guards never drew for us.
Cam asked about my weekend and if I have kids. I
said yeah 4- she says oh wow you look so young what
grades. I say I am almost 34. She says "Well that's still
young to have a highschooler."

9/13/22
The bullying is too much.
Tell your story.
Own the truth.

Part 2 title could be: street teach. Diary of a crossing guard part 2. (well, if you have this book in your hands, you know what I decided on for the name lol.)

Today like 20 or more, old school cop cars went by, towards the base.

I could write hello in different languages. Or other phrases.

I debated on staying home, because my youngest isn't feeling well.
But, here I am at work.
I know that she will be cared for and I know we are lacking crossguards and it's late notice.

9/14/22
Gratitude is my way of coping with many things.
Including grief.
I have heard: Doing the same thing over and over and expecting different results is insanity.
What worked one year, may not work for you anymore.
What do you have to lose in trying something new?
What different pivots have you had?
I want and need less busy life.

I want schools that care about my children, they aren't just another child with stuff going on- with no time for.
A face to get paid.

I do the behind the scenes and the bloopers. That's who I am, how I am and I love it about me. Hints, another reason why my books are imperfectly perfect.

9/15/22
"you are out here risking your life"

Even when you are sure, its not for sure.
Not sure until its for sure.

My hat fell in the street when I was on my bike. Things like this make me have to take extra time for the unexpected. Happy I got it back.

A woman walking shared she came back from visitng family in Alaska. "In Alaska it was so green , back here the green is yellow."

Little girls saw drawings "ooooh" "I love your drawings" Her big sister says "it was fun"---the crazy different hop scotches and things I put on the pathway.
I like the design, ive never seen it before- another girl said.

Today I need to talk about my anxiety. My kids walking. Knowing the work I do and the things I see. Nothing new but we should talk about it.

9/16/22
I helped a young girl get in the gate. The coast guard community has a locked gate and you need a code to get in. I am happy I was able to help. It makes me

think about how the specific crossguard at this site, should have that information to help this specific community. Some of the kids walk alone and sometimes the gate has issues.

A young boy is at the chalk drawing of moods/feelings and says "question mark means mystery. Maybe you can erase it and put a star face"
A young girl chose heart but said "im heartbroken"

A dad says "are you responsible for all of the chalk work?" " I appreciate it, especially any dad jokes. Mine aren't appreciated"

A mom says to her daughter"shes the one that does the chalk" daughters says loud "we love them" with a smile
The mom who made comments before says "told you we love them, it makes our day. We thought about bringing chalk to reply and add to." Kids say "yeah, lets."

There's a boy who walks alone. I asked him "did you learn anything new today? Anything fun?" He says division.
A child said division was fun! I love that!

My brother-in-law and nephew stopped by today.Moments like that really make my day because it was such a surprise.

My oldest daughter is home today with a higher than usual temperature. So of course I am concerned and can't wait to get home.

Why does she have a whistle? A 4 year old asks her mom.
Mom then asks me why do you have a whistle?
This was great a great conversation to ask the 4 year old their ideas. She was actually pretty spot on. I love hearing how childrens minds work.

I am thinking of stencils and how maybe they can help me create artwork.

9/19/22
Ideas rolling in this morning:
Monday funday.
Monday with chalk and jokes.
Magical Monday. What is magic?
Green light when you need it.
Thank you rain for.
Monday mood.

A fellow crossguard gave me a cookie. She wanted me to try her treats, she has her own baking business. Such a sweet gesture. And, it was delicious! I will definitley be buying some in the future.

Referring to the rain, "you have a new canvas" a family said "we get to see your new work." How are you on chalk? A mom asks.

A mom says "pretty easy for a Monday morning especially after rain."

A dad walked by and told me a joke. Whats green and fuzzy hurts if it falls? Trees? Pool table and hes says "well you aren't wrong"

Alaska lady came by again. "I am trying to go 3 times this year, to help my sister start another business." "I crossed the street this afternoon when you weren't here and it was crazy"

*As I look at the ground I think "if you fix all of the breaks and cracks- how will you be reminded about whats underneath? The story? The history?

9/20/22
I was writing and when I got up, a mom is standing at the gate of a playground. "are you writing messages?" I say yes. She says "oh thank you for that. I love it. Its so nice of you to do."
So far I always see her with her children playing, same time everyday- but they never come out the gate to cross.

The little boy who asked me to draw a star face, chose the star face today. He asked me last Friday morning if I could draw that and I put it that afternoon but then it rained. Today he noticed.

Another cross guard saw me and she says "are you listening to music" as I was riding on my path home. I say no. She says "oh I see your head moving."
I was singing and listening in my head lol

I have always known this job is what you make of it. But speaking with others I realize how unhappy and negative their experience is. And how easily it rubs off on me. So I already started taking distance. I realize even more it's what you make it. I could easily complain about so much as well but I choose to focus otherwise.

I saw a Snail, rollie pollie. Butterfly, ladybug. So many sites to see, things to learn.

As I observe the rollie pollie, so much comes to mind. I don't know if you want to hurt me or help me. So I retreat.
It took 20minutes for it to unroll.

What has my last year of life given me?
What do I want for 34?

People walking dogs so I keep my distance
Kids in cars with no car seats, no seatbelts. People on phones.
I can be crossing people in an empty street and a car can come speeding in the same moment.
A preganant woman walking her dog, thanked me. Because she didn't expect the help.

9/21/22

One mom said "no bike?" to me this morning. I love that people notice things, that I am cared for and seen and apprceiated.

I did chalk in the rain, people still stopped for it.

A little girl asked me "whats your favorite fruit?' when crossing. I was caught off guard and said "kiwi". Then I thought to myself, where did this come from? As in my answer, because it is rare that I eat Kiwi. I guess, a Kiwi sounds good to me right now-but it actually isn't my favorite. Why did I say that. Why does it matter what I said. It matters to me, because I want to say the truth, it was true at time but not really.

Today my husband gave me pepper spray.
Surprising enough, it may be needed one day.
That is a scary feeling and thought. And, I am happy to have this tiny piece of extra safety.

I noticed one boy not wearing his helmet today, he was walking his bike across and was happy I reminded him and he put it on before riding.

9/22/22

A guy walking with his pants down this afternoon...
Yep, thats what I said. Thats what I saw. He obviously was not fully mentally all there. Maybe drugs or something involved.
Times like this make me feel all kinds of ways like unsafe and my mind is racing on how to protect

children and myself. Luckily, this was a moment of no kids. And he didn't say anything to me, he just kept walking.

I pulled a muscle this morning on my bike ride. Situations like that are never fun but I will live , it just sucks.

Empty street, guy on bike got off to walk it "I figure since you ask the kids I should. " I told him I appreciate it.

I felt like I wasn't honest about fruit answer so let me explain...
when I saw the family again from yesterday.
Why am I so deep about everything?
I tell the mom my favorite fruit is plum , not that it matters but I want to be honest. Mom says "she wanted to buy you something that's why she asked"
I was so shocked I had no idea.
Then today she asks "whats your favorite dessert?"
I had no answer because we were in the middle of the street. I say "I like surprises"
I was inspired so I wrote the fruit question in chalk. I think she said hers is apple.

9/23/22
I was crossing people but a car in traffic said once they got to me. " you are doing an amzing job, keep it up."

9/26/22

Today a family of girls came close to the time I was leaving and the mom asks "how long are you out here?"
I'm sure people wonder my schedule, it's good to know and share.

Schools nearby have been off for the week.

My supervisor came this morning to switch out my stop sign, twice because it kept breaking.

A dad walking told a marathon joke. I love that this parent is sharing jokes with me, I know personally the time it takes to be intentional.

Whats your favorite magic trick?
What is magic?

9/27/22

A father says "you must get your steps in, all this back and forth."
Some moments feel more than others, thats for sure.

A young girl says her dog wants to ride my bike. That would be interesting.

9/28/22

A family walks by and the little girl is talking to her mom. Her mom says to me "she thinks you should be a teacher because you are very nice" I said I was one for about 7 years and she says "well there you go."

Boy on bike waits for people blocks away so they can open the gate for him. We talk while he's waiting and he says the good part about his day was drawing- no actually writing about our past self.
That sounds like a wonderful activity to partake in at school.

Kids and parents know my name. It feels good to be talked to by name, it makes me want to learn their names. But I do not want to cross any boundaries by asking.

9/29/22
A family drove by today, just so the kids could say hi and bye to me.
The same dad who told me jokes before, has another. A joke about numbered days and a calendar. I love that he shared this while in the car with his family. Some of them put their hands on their forehead, while others laughed lol.

There was a flying spider in the wind not even connected to a tree. Just flying in wind on a web.

Older man this morning in punch buggy asked me my name and shared his but I couldn't really hear him. He is such a nice person, I really want to know his name. I wonder if it'll ever happen..

9/30/22

Dad tells a joke about a printer "paper jamming" he says to me "the dad jokes you wrote are really highlights of parents days. We love it so thank you."

Little girl runs to me and asks me how I am and how was my day.

Little boy says he doesn't like walking his bike across the street, I agree it can be not fun when I do it as well but it's for safety I re-assure him. I am happy I got to let him know that he isn't alone with his feelings and still remind him why we do it.

My supervisor said "we need more lena's for this work."
What a kind thing to say.

Little girls asks where I live and Cam says "wow you ride all the way from park street?' they ask if I have weekend plans and I say maybe the pumpkin patch and she says them too. She says her kids want to go up the street but that's lame and we connect on wanting to go to a "real one" and how the kids are satisfied with these new aged jumpy house ones. Whos it really for? What is lame? What matters?

10/3/22

How am I making a difference?
You can smile at any job.

A truck slowed down, man and woman (cars behind)
says "you have a dangerous job" I say I do he says
"some people are just straight up a-holes"

I hear a mom telling her two kids the jokes. She asks if
I know the code to the gate.

A guy walking across says "you should have a shirt
with wings on it, see you smile away with the best
they'd stop looking at their phones."

10/4/22
Little girl at the gate with her mom scooter waiting for
me to wave, they never cross while I am here but I see
them come out to play – the same time, every day.

10/5/22
Several kids hugged a tree because of the writing
One little boy says "im going away today or tomorrow
so you wont see me for the next 4 days"
How beautiful that people want to share things with
me, even if it means nothing to others, it's such a gift.

10/6/22
When I close my eyes,
anxiety fills my mind
I am trying to use all the tools I have invested in
Drinks, programs, knowledge, people and practicies.
This job is so scary and crazy and dangerous.

10/7/22
I don't always remember to take notes about my experiences and days and times.
Today, is one of those days.
And, thats ok.

10/10/22
How many hearts can you find on your walk?
Why do we celebrate others and not ourselves? Why not? Why push me to the side? So I decide to open up. I put me in the open, opportunity to be noticed- comes with some fear.

Kids played couting hearts.

10/11/22
Just because its broken doesn't mean its not still what it is.
What are you feeding your mind?

"are you the one who does all the writing? We loooooooooove it"- someone said to me.

Please don't ask me how I am, cause I can't lie or be fully real right now. A conversation or small talk while crossing the street is not long enough. But silence would for sure feel way worse.

I saw a new family walking.

On my bike ride I saw a pile of needles, because it was near the school and bloody clothes were with it. I could

not, not do anything. So, I called the non emergency line, I just wanted it clean. I don't want the thoughts of thinking what if a child or someone picks something up. What if someone experiments or tries to clean it themselves and gets hurt. This is a situation where I feel like "if you see something, say something."
Happy to report, that after my shift- I did go to check if it was cleaned up-and it was.

10/12/22
This morning a boy said something to me in german. A word for goodbye. He said he heard his mom say it. This afternoon he asked if I remembered the word.

There is a little girl who always runs to me to say hi. I asked about her day. Do anything fun? She said River rocks as she picked up a tumbling leaf.
---triggered memories of having a rock tumbler when I was young and the things I created.

10/13/22
Goodbye in german, the same boy is still trying to teach me. I love that even as adults, we are forever learners. And to teach has no age , we can learn from anyone.

Everyone is cold today and seems surprised by it, I dressed warm- I learned from yesterday.

A lady walking by "why do you guys write on the path?" in rude way (it sounded to me) I say for fun. Her tone

sounded jugemental, first time I got that. And why say you guys, its just me and her here.
I can also be wrong. Maybe she wasn't being rude or judgemental. Maybe thats just her tone.

10/14/22
The day before my birthday .
I decided I will write in chalk for me, like I do for everyone else.
I'll admit, this took some courage. It took lots of talking myself into.
It's really not for the attention and it's not done with any expectations. The only expectation is to love myself the way I love others. To celebrate myself the way I would others.
The happy birthdays from people took me by surprise.

10/17/22
I saw a family I haven't seen in awhile. I said its nice to see you. She said you too, it'll be our last week. She said they are moving back home, to Indiana. I say i've seen it on tv. She says "it's what you see, its good- I realize I need to be with my husband because shes growing too fast", pointing to one of her daughters.
Well congratulations so happy for you that's beautiful.
She says "you have been a bright light here, so thank you"
What a gift for people to share any of their life with me. To be inspired by words and choices. I am so thankful.

Kids at work this morning "happy birthday again"

10/18/22

I hung a ghost on the tree next to the location I work at. The kids talked about what it was. Ghost or witch or both?
Did you bring that? Parents and kids asked.
I did take it back home, to bring it back tomorrow.

10/19/22

The woman and family moving to Indianna saw me again and she reminded me and thanked me for being a bright light for her during their time here. She said, See you next time.
I really want to give them a gift before they leave and hope to see them again.

Love , intention , effort.

A guy who works at jean sweeny asked "how many times do you go back and forth a day?" my name is B by the way

A guy walking his dog asks "whats the glue riddle?"The answer is on the side I tell him.
Answer: Stick with me and youll be fine.
I love how so many people read the jokes and what not and so many don't see the answers right there. It makes me happy that people are taking the time to try to figure it out.

10/20/22

"in England we call you the lollipop lady" a family says to me.

10/21/22

Work has me programmed to smile.
At least thats a thought that came to mind.
I see people, people who wave so I wave back and it's
just the easiest thing to do without even thinking- to
smile.
I notice how contagious smiles are. If I give one, 90%
of the time it comes back to me. If I get a smile, it's an
instant one for me.
This work, particularly-makes it easy to smile. (at least,
for me.)

10/24/22

My mother-in-law passed away, this
morning.

When a death happens, it should go without not
needing to think twice-that work just isn't priority.
Because, it's not.

And yet of course I am thinking of the kids who walk
alone and the families and how it's 3 in the morning
and I need to text my supervisor but also don't want to
text at this hour and also, don't want to wait for the last
minute.
So, by 6am I let him know what was going on and that
today I wouldn't be in. That I would also like to use any
sick time to make up the hours and pay.
He was very understanding.

10/25/22

I did not want to get up this morning, so tired, my body feels heavy.
I wrote in chalk for martha (my mother-in-law.)

"we missed you yesterday" I heard people say.
"kids were asking yesterday, did she move?" other families say.
"welcome back" everyone says.

It was as if I was gone for days, It had only been yesterday.
But, it is not like me to miss. Especially unexpectedly.
I am aware I mostly serve coast guard families and so sometimes peole come and go unexpectedly- I can see why they may have thought that of me as well.

Today is also a tough day , when it comes to the passing of my mother-in-law. I am needed with my family. So, although I was able to manage my morning shift. Due to the drive and time needing to be made this afternoon, I asked for the afternoon off as well. Luckily, this time- I was able to inform some of the families as I say thiem this morning.
I never told anyone why.
I didn't want to put that knowing on anyone.
I probably also am still realizing whats really real now and wanting to not accept it.

A father of my husbands friend from school has to start chemo and hes scared. I have so many emotions and thoughts. We try to be supportive. The best we can.

10/26/22

"where were you yesterday" a little boy asks. I had missed the afternoon shift and not everyone who walks in the afternoon walks in the morning, so I didn't see him.
I say, I was with my family.

A mom says "she was asking about you, concerned" talking about her daughter.

"will you wear your costume? I bet kids will love it" a parent says. I let her know I was already planning on it. I am happy that the thought isn't just mine, it makes me feel more excited to do it.

"you are risking your life" someone walking by says as they know this road can be dangerous more often than not.

A young girl yelled from car "be my teacher!"

"does it snow in California?"
"do race cars have headlights?"

10/27/22

A dad says "what is orange and sounds like a parrot …a carrot"

Lol

10/28/22

It's Friday, I came across a picture of my daughter (she was wearing her cookie monster onesie) and so- I asked to borrow it, so I could wear it to work this morning. I was so warm in that onesie and my vest fit over it just fine.

One little boy was with his sister and mom, out of the stroller this time. While crossing, his mom said "he picked you a flower" they waited until we got back to the sidewalk to give it to me.
That was so sweet and unexpected.

Several cars stopped to say "I like that" "I like your outfit" so many children and families filled with smiles. One little girl thought she was going to be the only one dressed up today and was happy to see me dressed up too. So many said "you look so warm today" "you look very snuggly"
"thank you for dressing up"

Am I the cookie monster in a crossing guard costume or a crossing guard in a cookie monster costume?

I say I like your outfit, not costume. Because who am I to say it's a costume to you.

10/31/22

Chalk work.
What is the longest a Disney short film can be, I have an idea.
Crosswalk, crossing guard, chalk.

Chalk work, cross walk, a short Disney film.

11/1/22
This is the second day a young boy, not in school yet-jumps out of his wagon to pick a face. (I have a section of expressions for some to share how they are feeling.) He jumps on the happy face "im this one." And his slightly older brother says "halloween is over, why is the pumpkin still there?" I say "well, november has some pumpkins too and it hasn't rained to wash it away yet."

11/2/22
As I was watching movies with the kids I thought about what if one day I can create a disney short film. With few or no words. About chalk writing and cross guard. Share how the idea came from a pandemic/masks and little time. Wanting to communicate and engage community while spreading joy.

11/3/22
I crossed an adult and he made a comment "do you need the practice?" I said this is my job for an hour, so this is what I do. Then he says thank you.

11/4/22
While doing this job, I see people I used to know. Some from school or work. We don't always notice eachother. With my hair up and uniform , I don't think they would really notice me in passing anyways with how fast moving it is.

But, I start to think...I wonder what they think, if they
see me.

If you pass me and knew me in highschool or as a
teacher, I wonder what you think.
Don't think I am not happy.
I chose this job and it chose me.

11/7/22
I don't want someone to get hurt in order for change.
But that is how I am feeling, that this road and section
will have no change until something bad enough
happens to create that change.
It upsets me so much that this world works in that way.
I hope it never comes ot that.

11/8/22
The grief sneaks up randomly.
The tears fall, randomly.
Try to find a moment for no one to see,
at least not while I am working.

11/9/22
A mother asks her daughter "what are you feeling
today?" as they stop at the drawn faces. Her child
chose the crying face and mom asks why and she
says "because today I cried a lot."

11/10/22
So many roads blocked off, forcing me to go different
ways on my bike. Different paths to explore. I feel like I

am gambling with time, unsure of how long different paths will take. Trying to make it to work on time.

Drawing with wet chalk, realizing the piece of chalk goes away fatser but as it dries- it looks the same as when writing with dry chalk.

I write the reminder no school Friday and modified days all next week.

One kid chose sad face just to see parents reaction. She said that and laughed when dad got concerned.

11/11/22
No work no school no pay
But hey, time to enjoy the day.

Thankful to have a job. Thankful to have the day off. Thankful to feel grateful.

11/14/22
I commented on a young girls jacket, how warm it looked. Her mom says "if only I could get her to wear pants."
And I said "we take the wins where we can."
We both laughed and agreed on different things. I can definitley relate to what she had said.

It makes me reflect on my children and my thoughts as a parent.

Our children know themselves. We can be open to trusting that they know and they will tell us when they need or want something.

We think we know whats best (and as adults/parents/guides, I beleieve we do at times.) I also think about how peole have tried to tell me whats best for me at times and I undesrtand it comes from a good place- but whats best to one might not be the best to someone else.

A guy walking says "thanks for doing this. I live close by and always see it. We love this, how did you get inspired to do this?" I explained the pandemic inspired me. Wanting to connect beyond the cross walk and masks and fears. To help invite play and joy.

I was on my way home and I hear a mom say to her child "we are too late" and when I look she says "he is asking why you are leaving. He's just confused."
I was only two blocks away from my job location,so I biked back to cross them.
She was so appreciative. And the cars were so fast- she was extra grateful "see, glad we had you here."
It didn't take much more of my time to stay the xtra couple of minutes. I am happy I did it.

11/15/22
"thank you , we enjoy all of the jokes" A family member visitng says.

"I love the puns you put out. The fish one made me giggle. I know its for the kids but I love them." A mom says.
I let her know, it's for everyone- even myself. And thank her.

11/16/22
As people pass and some share words. I think to myself how we never know whose story we will get to be a part of. So many of these people are a part of mine in some way. Some consistent with this job position.
But also so many have shared about me and chalk work and how they share with their families and friends.
You just never know how you and your impact goes beyond you. Might not ever know.

11/17/22

11/18/22
A family of 3 girls who walk to school in the morning, have their dog. The dog pooped and the youngest girl asks her mom "why is smoke coming from the poop?" it was 44 degress out.

So, I ask you- why was there smoke?

No work 11/21-2(until 28)

11/28/22

This man who has started walking by in the mornings
says "I was a crossing guard for two years. I only
stopped because I started to work for the district."

I crossed a family of women this afternoon and the
older woman says "doesn't it get lonely out here?"
I was almost off, it was pretty empty.
But I told her its great time to reflect.
The other woman who I assume might be her daughter
screams "yes!!! Time for me myself and I."
they all tell me to be safe because its dangerous.

11/29/22

I noticed a woman walking towards me, someone I
have seen in the community but have not crossed. As
she gets closer I do get ready to ask if she will be
crossing so I can prepare to help. Before I can say
anything she says "oh im not crossing. I just wanted to
give you this gift. We really love all of the quotes and
walk around just to see them. Thank you. It's a box of
quotes"

Is it cause I haven't been chalking?
How does she know it's me, has she seen me?
I will definitley use these to inspire my chalk creations.

A woman walking dogs was surprised I went to cross
her "oh you cross anyone?"

11/30/22

I was chalking this afternoon and a woman walking by in a mask said "oh wow! I always wondered who writes these and now I know. I love them. Thank you so much"

12/1/22

So many driving, so many kids not buckled. I see this all the time and I am so concerned. I hope to never hear any bad situation take place. I feel like I am no one to speak up and also who am I not to.

12/2/22

I was excited to wake up to pay day and pay bills. I went on to paycor to check my check and it was a lot smaller than I expected. I forgot break effects this pay day. I did what I could and then shifted my focus to some happier thoughts.

Today is my oldest brothers birthday and he is coming to visit. Thank goodness it's Friday.

Reminded myself why I love this work and that I also love what I get paid.

As I draw some faces with chalk this morning I start to think about *options.*
Do you prefer less options or more? To choose from? Would you know your options if they weren't laid out? (if the options of faces weren't here, would you choose from whats available or would you ask for whats

missing if it did not resonate---this thought can go for many things in life.)

A child walks by and says to her parents "my day was like this emoji" dad says "this emoji?" making the same face.

A mail lady I have not seen drove by and said "thank you for all you do"
I wonder what she means exactly.
Not that she has to mean anything in particular. Could just be a nice comment.

A young girl walking with her dad tried to tell me a joke but there wasn't enough time when crossing. Her dad tells me jokes all the time. I love that she wants to now as well.

12/5/22
Young girls yells from car "take me home, be my mommy." I know she is just playing and although a little akward, I am sure it's all sweet intention.
I don't mind, kids will be kids. I hope her parents never feel any type of way. I just take it as, kids will be kids and they are unpredictable lol.

12/5/22
This morning a little girl said to her dad "can I tell her?" then she comes up to me and says "I am going to Sweden in 9 days." Then pulls out a purse toy and asks "do you like it?"

I do like it of course, I thank her for sharing and wish them safe travles and lots of fun.

A guy riding by on a bike looks up and says "I see a grin of heaven" pointing to the sky. "im Michael"

12/7/22
Today is the first Wednesday of the month which means it's extra early release date. I start by 11:45.

I say "good-afternoon" to a mother walking, Cam says "barley lol I wish they would keep the kids longer. Its not much time to get anything done."
I totally hear you, I get home just to come right back. I do like it though, having more of my day after I get done here.

A father was the last to cross this morning before I was off. He realized I was waiting to cross him and says " oh I thought the vip treatment was only for the children."

Many comments of "stay warm" this morning from people walking and driving.

One father came out in shorts in the cold—he said "well, it was warm in the house."

This mornings fun was smoke coming from the pile of woodchips that was just placed.
Fresh woodchips, cold morning=smoke and so many interested curious kids.

I love conversation starters like this. Things to get the mind working.

12/8/22
It's Thursday. I got a ride to work this morning.
A grandfather walking children to school says "it's beautiful here" I say yes it is, right now. It was a beautiful moment. He laughed and agreed.
I wonder where he is visitng from.

In the afternnon A man saw me biking to work and said "thanks for doing that work"

12/9/22
Not all crossing guard positions pay the same price. Different locations have differences in pay.
I learned this when I thought we were moving.
Why is that so?

Why do we ask you to walk your bikes and scooters when we cross you?

1/9/23
Back from winter break
I crossed 8 people this morning. Probably due to the rain and flood warnings, high winds. I biked in this, it wasn't too bad. I dressed warm enough but my tea was cold by the time I got to work.

Some students walk alone, so I am happy I showed up.

More people walked in the afternoon, thanks to the no rain and it not being cold. It is crazy and very different, amazing what a few hours can do.

"Hi ms lena I read what you wrote and something I did over winter break was go to the great wolf lodge"
her brother says "we are going on a cruise."

So many happy people waving from cars.

"i'm good you don't have to cross me, im not a kid, im 27, how old do I look?" but I cross them anyways and they say Thank you.

1/10/23
You point=view point

1/11/23
I got a ride this morning. It's my brothers birthday. Flooded memories. Almost tears.

It's another day of the big gate being open, and this means extra traffic.
For a few minutes a cop parked and traffic was well behaved and I felt happy.

So many cars pass and wave, kids roll down windows to talk or speak or listen.

1/12/23
No rain, lots more people walking this afternoon.

"she is very concerned about you in the rain." A parent says to me. Her little brother said "be my teacher" the little girl asks if she can touch my sign. And then says "look at my scooter I got it for Christmas. Is that bird poop?" she asks on my sign.

Tree with weird leaves.
Wet chalk work.

Woman in car "thank you for all the work you do. do you like chocolate? I am going to make you some"

People driving by "thank you for what you do"

1/13/23
Life just keeps moving
How are you moving along?

1/16/23
Monday no school.

I wish I knew...

1/17/23
Healing has no time limit, no directions, no one size fits all. It's a journey

Parent "oh yay chalk art is back"

Little girl asks me "how much chalk do you have? How do you have enough to do all this? Do you have lots more?

One child says look my tooth fell out.
I am reminded about how natural it comes to children,
to want to share about themselves.

Kids who walk alone are into the jokes and hopscotch
Lots of people crossing today, new faces too.

An older couple was walking around , reading all the
chalk.

A woman walking by asked if I knew about any free
food services. I let her know about the food bank and
how it was close by.

A young girl asked me if I could speak spanish.
Because I had written some things but I told her no, I
wish I knew.

1/18/23
What feelings do you need to sit with right now?

"well that's above and beyond" a mom says.
A husband and wife and twins were crossing the
street. The twins, 1 boy and 1 girl. As they are crossing
I hear the young girl say she dropped her flower. A
pink flower, she really wanted to go back to get it. Her
parents were wanting to continue walking home. I was
already crossing back to the side of the street where
the flower was so I decided to pick it up and give it to
her. I wanted to make the parents walk home happier
and the child's mood happier.

In my mind, it costs nothing to be kind. I responded with "it's something very small of me to do, to help bring a smile, no problem at all."
Doesn't cost me money, time or anything. The road was clear, my shift was almost over.

A parent walking shares her fears and worries with me. "It's me again but this time I left my daughter alone. I like to walk but she doesn't and it takes an hour to walk back and forth. I hope she's ok."

1/19/23
Whos deadline is it
What can wait.
Who are you?
Who are you meant to be?

How many times does 3 go into 6? What is 6 divided by 3? 2x3
You can ask a question in different ways and get the same answer

You did it! What did you do? Or get done. Or feel good about today.
Celebrate yourself.

1/20/23
A little boy says "and by the way, my birthday is Monday. I will be 9!"

Two boys locked in the gate, I couldn't open it. Someone eventually comes and says "you have to put all your weight on it to get in."

A little boy walking with his mom says at his school they are selling popcorn and poscicles today, he is excited. He tells me they are each $1. I give him two dollars and ask if he can buy something for someone who wants it, because I will be gone from work by then and I just want to support the fundraiser. He gives me two start stickers as a thank you.

A little girl wanted to hug me and got upset because it couldn't happen right in the middle of the street. Once we crossed, she even gave my husband a hug.

So many people crossing today.

1/23/23
I could see a family coming from their home. They have a long enough walk before getting to me, that I notice the daughter in a pumpkin costume.
So, I quickly make a drawing with chalk. Of a pumpkin.

A mom points and says loudly "WHAT!!!" to a picture drawn, while walking with her kids. She follows it by "that's a funny coincidence!!"

Another mom and daughter crossing, daughter is in a pumpkin dress and the mother says "it's like she knew"

Three kidsare walking and share it's someones birthday. One child says "why is there a pumpkin, it's not Halloween"

1/24/23
I heard afamily saying it was a childs birthday this morning. So, I wrote happy birthday this afternoon and the child noticed and said to her parents „how did she know?" with excitement in her voice. As if it was magic. Such a beautiful moment to be able to see and hear.

1/25/23
A young boy asked me "do you come in the morning, did someone give you stickers(he did , earlier and he noticed it on my stop sign), can you redraw the snail."

You look so beautiful someone said to me.

Maybe they can draw a sun for the nice days, pumpkin Is out of season- a woman says to the kids she is watching.

A lady driving stops at corner and asks how am I, "did you like the chocolates? Oh good. I don't have young children anymore but I see all the work you do. You bring the neighborhood so much joy. We really appreciate all you do"

1/26/23
Why do I do diary/poetry/journals? Well, for me, I then feel like I don't need to hire big editors- I choose not to.

Diary and poetry feels real and authentic and it's why I am ok with errors.
I am glad my dads new book is taking time because now I get to add my 9 year reflections in.

I am Manifesting seeing you more.

A girl thought my hand was broken because of my glove, she was so concerned. I showed her it's just a glove and she felt better.

1/27/23
What has this job taught me today? Or, so far?
(this question can be for you as well- in your life to reflect on.)

What are the lessons from today.

What are some things I want to remember?

1/30/23
This morning, a man crossing had his dog on a leashe but the whole collar came off
Luckily I was able to use my stop sign and stoop low so that the dog didn't run into the street.
He was able to calm the dog down and get everything back on him.
He thanked me for my help.

I am thankful I was able, this road is so scary- things could have gone differently and I am so happy it went well.

1/31/23

Do you know what these symbols mean? I was
thinking of chalking, writing some symbols. These days
so much has changed, where we put our attention.

A little girl rode ahead of the family to talk to me, the
little girl wore her duck costume. She inspired me to
draw ducks with chalk.
"how do you draw a duck?" a she asks me, looking at
the one I drew. I say-do you want to try? She says yes,
so I give her chalk. She draws. Her faily gets to her
and says how amazing her drawing it (it was really
good.)
The other day her sister said "wear a different costume
everyday to see if it gets drawn"

2/1/23

I want to create "just because cards"
There will always be new stress, new challenge, new
fear. You gotta learn to be right here.
Too often we see people drowning but the moment we
see their head above water we turn away. Like they
are ok enough.
Well, I want people to know when they are being seen
and that they are appreciated.

2/2/23

A boy said "you are good at your job"
I wonder what makes me good at it, to him

A guy walking says "can I ask you a question? Do you
know sterling? He works in Berkeley. All I know is you

mentioned your husband and I mentioned it to him and he says he knows oyu both". I say yes I know him, we all went to school together. Well this person turned out to be relative of his. What a small world. It feels good to be know and to know others. It makes me feel a bit safer out here.

"I got a skateboard for my birthday yesterday and now I am 11. I am older" one child shared. Her brother shared as well, they are twins.

"can I ask, did you work all that time it was raining?" rain or shine I say

"sorry, have to go back for backpack" someone said as I had crossed them but they came right back.
Why do we say sorry about things like this?
I am guilty of it, ae you?

Why do you wear a hat? Someone asked me.

_2/6/23_
This morning there wasn't any chalk left around because of the rain on Friday.
A little girl remembers where the faces used to be and says I feel "snail and happy."

This afternoon I drew with chalk .
A grandma asks "what makes you happy?" and the little girl says "you."
A grandpa says look I can hopscotch too.

A man walking by says "they will put lights one day here cause they need to, how can they not. But then i'm sorry youll lose your job, those cars go too fast"

I was able tp help a boy who fell off his bike. That situation made me extra happy I had just asked him to wike his bike across. Can you imagine if he was riding and fell in the street?

A guy told me hes the son of god, that a woman denied him but not me. Cause the chosen see the chosen and light see light. He says a girl kicked him out but hes ok cause the script was written .

2/7/23
Happy 1 year hired as crossing guard Lena.
I wrote this in chalk, to celebrate myself.

why celebrate? why not. I do love this job.
and this past year has taught me so much and given me so much.

Saying yes to that job posting on indeed was not as quick and easy as it sounds.
I applied, twice.
because I wanted to secure income. It was a job that didn't require certain things other places were. It had consistent yet flexible hours.
It was "good" income. As in the pay was great to me and I could help with our bills.

I wanted this particular job for more reasons than just income.
I had been working from home and screens all pandemic.
This would get me back out, into the world, in work-in this way.
I would get to work with families and kids again, in a sense.
I would get to be outside, fresh air.
I get to learn a new role.
I get to bike to work and get exercise.
I would have same days off as the kids.

It came with challenge.
"but it isn't enough money"
you don't get paid holidays and days off like as a teacher.
I would need to find a babysitter for athena.

For my start, the first five months, our kids were still in online school. Babysitter covered.
all income was helpful.

I quickly made connections. Beyond masks and 6 feet and fears.
I used chalk to create opportunities for fun, learning, conversation, connection and curiosity.
The chalk art work has stuck with me, even a year later.

I refused moving to other locations.
I turned down the ask to be a supervisor.

I have enjoyed almost two different school years now, although in 1 year.....

because of this job I have found ways to be in joy and spread joy.
It has supported me in living in my alignment and purpose.
I created a book thanks to the experience and am working on another.
I have been given gifts in so many ways.
my husband and I have made time for us during car rides and walks.

I have faced fears. when it comes to standing in my truth, doing what I said I would, I found a commitment that's unshakable and yet still reminding me that jobs are jobs and the rest such as happiness and health are first priority.

biking has helped me drink more water, enjoy warm tea, push myself physically and mentally. I have made time for music and podcasts. I have had some great thoughts and writings come to me during my time on the bike or while doing my job.

This job has given me, so much of me back.
but i had to look for what I felt called to. I never went looking for this job but once I read it, I knew in my heart....
Then I had to do all the steps to "get it" and train and start.

and then show up.
I chose into this experience and I choose what this experience will be for me.
I am so thankful and happy and proud of my time here.

and I can't wait to finally be able to put in my request for my rain gear tomorrow.

2/8/23
Dear spark within...

2/9/23
Today I decided to do something I have thought about a bit before, I left chalk appreciation on a corner where an elder man is a crossing guard.

Then I left messages for drivers and walkers in that area which is not really near where I crossguard (not if you are walking).
Maybe it will inspire others.

I wonder if it will bring joy to his day.
It has to mine.
Through my mind of what if and through my heart of what is.
What ive seen and know to be true.
Maybe those who walk this path will too.
Even if I don't get to see.
I can still picture reality.

This morning is my first time of 5 days without feet warmers. My toes are frozen. There is a difference.

New families from different directions today. One looking for an orange toy from their walk yesterday . So many enjoying chalk jokes and riddles and affirmations.

2/10/23

I enjoy being a cross guard. I enjoy what it sparks in me. I enjoy with my role and how it sparks things in others.

Dear spark within
You've been dim
So committed to my commitments
That I show up regardless
But I am aware that I want my commitment to look and feel different

(Today I am choosing to miss in person yoga and osw, two things I have been chasing since 2021.)
I have to remember why I want it.
And how I want to show up in spaces that mean so much to me.
What I want to recieve in those spaces.

And to give myself grace if it isn't feeling right.
Remind myself that its ok to take a break.

Not feeling like yourself is a valid enough reason to take a day off or step back. You don't have to be sick in order to have reason enough to say you can't show up today.

There is so much on my to do list
And yet nothing I want to do.

I have felt this feeling before,
depression...

2/13/23
Be in your mess,
be with it

then, go live your best life

2/14/23
Oh hello valentines day. I love that someone I have
made friends with makes magic in her kitchen and I
can order treats for my family to celebrate the day. I
love supporting local, good people. I love connections.
I love trades. I love, love.

2/15/23
A little girl fell before crossing. She had on a skirt that
reminded me of a princess, so I googled a princess but
didn't have enough time to draw it before she went by.
Her mom was carrying her. I had time to draw before
they walked back this way.
When she walked back, she stopped and looks. I hear
her mom say "is that you?"

I eventually drew a prince as well. Because, why not.
Several children stopped with plenty to say, some with
no words.

A parent stopped to ask me if I drew the prince and princess and said that they are soooo good.

I checked in with a few kids who walk alone and a few parents just to let them know I wont be here this afternoon. They appreciated that.

2/16/23
I am so cold
But I tell myself I don't have to be
If everything is a choice
Then does that mean I am choosing?

Choosing to be cold, because that is what I am feeling...

2/17/23
The concept of gratitude , of being grateful
Is not to avoid or deny real feelings

2/23/23
Why does it have no eyes? Its creepy.
Maybe its mike wasouwsky with one eye?

2/27/23
Guy this morning "can I take a picture of you?" "we don't have this back at home in England" His daughter says sorry my family is visitng.

Meltdown, boy on scooter/street.

Big emotions cause want to be heard. Want to be listened to. Want to do what I want to do.

2/28/23

If the sun is there regardless
Then it's just the clouds creating shade
So lets get a fan and blow them away

Because I want more sun
I can see it
But can't feel it the way I wish I did

3/1/23

As I was getting ready to write, a Lady walking a dog "hi how are you? I really want to thank you from the bottom of my heart, for all the hard work you do. My husband sees you out in the cold, I am in the car and cant talk much when I see you but for so long I have wanted to tell you that God sees you and hears you. He is working on your behalf. He knows your struggles. You , your husband and kids. Give it to him. He is here for you. Those chocolates and this message is from him. Anytime you need a prayer I am here for you."
I cried

3/2/23

The language between cars is fascinating.
The signals, sounds, lights....

More hopscotch but not normal. More fun. With twists and turns and shades and "invitations/instructions."

"are those your boyfriends" the elderly guys that say hi.

A mom says she is trying to hussle across.
Another mom with son and a dog apologizes for being slow. Saying how they are always slow unless they use the stroller.
Another person with several dogs apologizes for being slower today than other days.

A family who usually passes enjoyed the spanish today. Didn't rush to cross. Stayed to do the how are you feeling.

3/3/23
5 deep breaths, 3 gratitudes right now, 1 intention for the day .

3/6/23
A leashe
Because I own you
A leashe
To keep you safe
A leashe
To have control
A leashe
To nudge you when you stop or slow down
A leashe
To guide you
A leashe, or lease?

(thoughts that came to mind as I watch pet owners walking their dogs.)

3/7/23
This morning a man, without any kids or anything. Stopped to say he appreciates me and to thank me.

3/8/23
My thoughts are important, powerful and valuable

3/9/23
I am not ignorning, I am just not allowing.

3/10/23
The amount of children and pets that stop in the middle of the street, amazes me.
When I say stop, I mean like stop. Lay down, get distracted by sights, wave at cars or whatever the case lol.

God blessed me with the courage to be myself.
You inconsistently consistently tried.
You aren't the one who will live with the regrets.

3/13/23
Someone stopped to tell me that I am the watcher of the children and they are so happy I am here and that they appreciate me.

3/14/23
I am a collector, in so many areas and aspects of my life.

Sometimes you have to be careful with what you collect.

3/15/23
I only worked the morning, truck in the way.

3/16/23
"how long do you stay out here?"
"how do people cross if you aren't here?"
Today I worked twice, thank you so much for working.

3/17/23

3/20/23.
I finally did it. Wrote in my "just because card" and waited for the car to give it. I had so many scenarios playing in my mind of how this could possibly go, while knowing it may not. This morning was a morning of extra stillness in the streets, so I was singing and praying for it to work out. 8:10 my husband came at just the right time, 1 girl crossing at just the right time. He was the second car, my husband with a hurt foot rushed to help me. I held the street as long as I could. And it worked out. Today was a rare morning that the same car drove back past me 8:24. Never usually see him twice, happened once before.

A friend is resigning.
Kids concerned telling me to be safe.
4 legged dog hold joke cause guy walking dog.

3/21/23

Rain. So thankful for the rain jacket my uncle lu gave me two days ago.
One car stopped and said are you ok.
So many children walking alone today, so many families.
I dropped my hat in street but was able to get it back luckily.

3/22/23

It is not often that I take long showers but this afternoon I got home and I was freezing. Soaking wet. It took 30minutes in the hot shower to even get color back into my hands and even start to feel them again.

I weighed my clothes before getting in the shower, 11 pounds! Of extra weight I was carrying home, on my bike ride and walk.

My 4 year old saying mom I told oyu not to go out there.

I am thankful my cousin was able to get me at 4:17 with his truck. I was not too far from home but in this wind and rain, it was very far away.

3/23/23

The punch buggy guy drove by and said "I love the card"
Guy working at jean sweeny said right after I passed by a big tree part fell and he was worried about me.

3/24/23

Dream vision manifest.
I want to guide and protect not pressure, influence with
guilt or shame or fear

3/27/23

Language of signs. Language of cars. Power of a stop
sign. Language of lights.

3/28/23

Being who you were,
isn't who you are

3/29/23

This morning I got a ride, it was raining. I was there by
7:15 to meet my site supervisor at 7:20, who didn't
show up until 7:31. The rain gear was heavy duty, just
a long jacket with detachable hat. Smells like plastic.
He tells me not to tell anyone else where I got it
because he doesn't have enough for everyone.
This afternoon it was sprinkly but 15 minutes in that
turned into rain and lots of hail. I was wondering why
the rain hitting my face hurt more than usual.
A little girl walking with her dad, ran to me and put the
umbrella over me. A boy in the passenger driving with
family saw the snowman, or maybe not and drew a
happy face on the window to me. A dad and his two
daughters drove by, they were at the corner waiting to
turn so I grabbed a snowball I made, tossed it in the air
and we wathed it drop , she laughed and smiled. A
young woman from Michigan said shes used to snow,
and said she can't believe she isn't escaping it. Shes

picking up two kids who usually get picked up by their parents, dog sometimes. A girl and her mom, who doesn't usually engage with the chalk writings, screamed with excitement about the snowman I made. A father and two sons drove by and the boys rolled down the window to say hi, "look a hail snowman" I am enjoying the cup their mom made me, it kept my tea warm the whole afternoon.
There were times this afternoon I wanted so badly to pour the warm tea on my hands to warm up.
3/30/23

3/31/23
Every now and then, a long line of police cars drive by. I wonder what they do.

4/3/23
I saw the punch buggy guy in a new car...
Well thats unusual.

4/4/23
Days, weeks, moments can be tough. I am proud of you-for doing the things.
Any of the things.

Chalk work can be simple.
Sometimes just a simple notice you and you are great as you are- goes a long way.

4/5/23
How do you balance work and life outside of it?

4/6/23

Cam says "Have you seen pip go by? I love that I know some by name and that families can check in with me and I can support.

A mom walking says she is so thankful i am here or else they would still be waiting to cross. I love that people and families know me by name.

4/7/23

Possibilities open up as oyu get shifts in your routine and time.
What will you create?

4/8-16 spring break

4/17/23

Back to it,
Feeling recharged and overflowing with inspiration
Hello Monday.
Mood, motivation, music, movement, money, mom, memories, miracles, moments,meals, meditation...
In 15 seconds or less what "m" words come to mind that matter to you?
When I hear parents and children answering questions or participating in the chalk work activities, it is soul-fulfilling. It's a bonus of heart work

4/18/23

This morning has been very busy and crazy. One mom was assertive in her voice and loud to a driver "there are children crossing, this is a 25 mile zone you know slow down!" I thanked her for standing up for us all and speaking out, this is not the first time.

4/19/23
A car see's another fast car, not stop for me or pedestrians and he says "that was exhilarating" with a smile but also concern in his voice.
my anxiety is higher today, I am not excited but at least others see what goes on at times.

4/20/23
I want to write letters to my kids. Inspired by so much everyday.

4/21/23
One boy said "today is my prom"- he was very excited, so why not be excited for him. Match that energy.
You never know how your energy can attach to someones day.

4/24/23
"he loved the facts about eels" sometimes when he is just chatting so much about something it's because he is interested. I replied, I don't ever hear kids or anyone talk about eels so it made me curious and I wasn't sure why it was on his mind but wanted to show I was listening and wanted to make it more interesting."
I noticed some kids in pajamas this morning so I asked, is it just a fun day or is it spirit week? Spirit week? I would like to try to participate so I asked a parent for the info for the week, they glady shared and were excited I wanted to join.

4/25/23

Today is "superhero day, you are super smart. Wear your super hero shirt" was the message from the school to families.

This morning I wore my army beanie, sweats and shoes because heros don't always wear capes and the community I mostly serve are cross guard families. This afternoon I decided to wear my batman leggings because any shirt will mostly be covered by my work vest. So many children stopped to say "hi batman/batgirl." A mom says "did you dress up because of spirit week?" As I arrived this morning, I noticed the sign that usually divides the two lanes was knocked off and to the side "state law, yield to people crossing within crosswalk." Although a rather small sign that doesn't always "help", I did feel less safe without it there.

As kids, of all ages crossed- I asked when I had time "who is your favorite super hero? Do you have a favorite super hero?"

Inspired by todays spirit day, I did some chalk work around everyday heros.

4/26/23

A younger child whos older brother once asked if I could draw a robot and dragon- said "draw a snake". His mother helped him reframe that into a question. "They sure know how to demand." Because I was working at this time, I couldn't draw but my husband who was on a walk arrived 5 minutes before my shift was ending and that particular family just a block and a half away. He quickly grabbed a piece of chalk from the car and drew a snake, because I asked.

I thought a lot today about how my uncle taught me early on "the squeacky wheel gets the oil"= "if you don't ask you'll never know. And when you ask- you will get an answer, nomatter what it is.

The little boy and other children were so excited to see the snake. "she drew it!!" I pointed and said "well, actually he did." I love that my husband got to feel some of that magic of chalk work.

Today is "team up and bring home the win! Wear your team gear"

This afternoon I was so excited and accomplished wearing spirit gear, I was several blocks away before realizing I forgot my vest. So I had to go back and get it.

4/27/23

Today for spirit week it is "our future is bright- wear sunglasses and bright colors."

Are you going to wait to cross more people who are a mile away?

A father says "I heard what happened the other morning, how a car just flew right past you"

What did the janitor say when he jumped out of the closet? Supplies. Daughter thought he said boo? Dad said it's a play on word for surprise.

They saw a car turn before I made it across.

I like your mustache, on my glasses.

Don't thank me yet, until we make it across.

4/28/23

Today for spirit week the invitation is "wear any Ruby gear or school colors.

Kids excited this morning to tell me they are going on a field trip, on the ferry!!!

A mom said this morning "I remember people saying last year having surveys of what would make this street better and safer but they've done nothing"

So many children and families went on field trip today, to the Exploratorium in sf, ..."

5/1/23

Mom and two girls crossing this morning "we tried to cross without you earlier and 3 cars wouldn't stop for us."

Dad walking by this afternoon "we appreciate you out here when it's not so fun. It's never something you see or hear about, someone making joy and finding fun on days of cold California when it hails making a snowman for the kids. I have a joke for you." computer, son, data

A mom crossing without me said she crossed 4 times earlier and people wouldn't stop for her.

5/2/23

This morning I got a ride to work but this afternoon I biked. I saw a hummingbird this morning and a turkey cross.

A boy found a snail and threw it. Do snails live in their homes?

What spirit day brought you the most joy? Instead of what was your favorite

5/3/23

This morning I got a ride to work. Today a boy passed on a bike "look what I found" he holds out a snail and then throws it into the grass.

This afternoon, I biked to work and two young girls ran ahead of their parents and said they were waiting. So I asked if they wanted to use chalk while they wait. They both screamed and jumped with excitement. They both drew fish, one named theirs "lucky."

5/4/23butterfly headband, no reason why, it was there so why not. First highschool boy "I like your headband" towards the end, another "I love your butterfly." Others commented and I would say thanks its my daughters.

So much mario excitement. Easier to see in the morning on wet dark ground. My husband seen and felt the community excitement. A request for him to draw peach and toad.

Sign in the middle of the road completely off from nail roots. Dragged down the street.

"almost friyay" a young boy says.

This morning I got a ride. My husband helped me draw. Mario figures, last night he said in the squares? Wasn't my intention but great idea.

I wore

5/5/23

A boy walking with his dad said about the mario characters "I think a guy drew these? Dad asks why. I think thats a big assumption but he's not wrong, my husband drew them. I am amazed.

5/8/23

Today I got a ride both shifts. This morning, all the chalk work is gone except rainbow. Kids are taking pictures with mario drawings. And a request for donkey kong. "He should be a tattoo artist"
Sign still not fixed.
In the afternnon, the sign in the middle of the street is gone.
A father walking says "did you hear/see?" I didn't understand. He shares the steam program at the school is in danger. That him and his family wont be here next school year, they are moving to west virgina but how we need people still here to raise he##. He says "you know what boggles my mind? Why is the gate closed when it can't be locked? And why don't teachers have money for school supplies? He was taking them some supplies.
Two kids walking say "will you draw the mario characters again? Especially bowser?"

5/9/23

"I really love what you do. Do you even know what a difference you are making? Sometimes kids are bored and they love this. My daughter asks for me to roll down the window when we drive just to see you. You should make an istagram"
I say I made one. She says "you should tell everyone about it, be proud. Can I follow you?" "I am constantly taking pictures of everything you do because we don't have this back in England."

A lady passing says "I love all of this. We appreciate it."
Person running wth their dog "I love what you are doing"
Guy driving by "what are you drawing today?"

5/10/23
A mom to me "we have a challenge if you choose to accept it…Donkey Kong." My husband says "challenge accepted"
"The sprinklers went on where you drew Yoshi and my son is going to be sad."
Are you a tattoo artist, they ask my husband.
I am trying to see it….I believe it, if oyu believe it.
"why didn't you draw luigi? Why didn't he?"

5/11/23
I noticed a mom who started following me on ig, might be a party planner.
Its Thursday, Tuesday my cup holder broke and today my cell phone holder.
Boy says I forgot to tell you weeks ago I learned to bike with no hands
A mom says thank you for happy birthday chalk writing

5/12/23
Today a bicyclist decided to continue moving forward as I was still in the street (stopping the traffic from his direction particularly.) I was crossing someone, a woman and stroller. Well, the card behind that bycyclist followed the bike. I am shaking my head no, stop sign and voice saying stop- blow whistle. While

the car continued to slowly go past me, in the street. I am saying loudly "what are you doing?" It was as if they pretended not to understand English or language of the roads, just because the woman and strolled had made it to the other side.

"Donkey Kong was perfect, the kids loved it. "

A young boy and his mom gave me flowers.

Lady I have been waiting to see, stopped at the corner today to say hi while she was driving by – I say "wait I have something for you."running to my bike I grab the card and book to give to her. She doesn't even know what it is and she says "you really made my day, GOD never gets it wrong." I tell her I have been waiting and hoping to see her, so happy I did.

I said happy mothers day to a mom driving, her daughter says its not mothers day its Sunday. I said but I wont see you on Sunday. She asks if I am a mom, I say yes to 4, she was shocked.
Boy says see you later like 6pm when I walk back across.

5/15/23
Would you rather swim through spaghetti or chocolate?
3 boys same grade all answered differently, talking through why they chose what they did.
Two said spaghetti and 1 said chocolate. Spaghetti cause easier cause liquid. You can walk on spaghetti.

A mom says spaghteeti because she would eat all the chocolate. Her son says well is the chocolate hard or thick.
Dad with 3 kids- kids said spaghetti, he says their answeres surprised him.
Mom and two kids. Kids said chocolate cause don't like spaghetti. She says well we are having pasta for dinner. Son says but that's ravioli.

5/16/23
No competition. Just collabortaions, connection, community.

"did you make the drawings all the way to ruby bridges? There were bright stars!"
----I did, we did. My family and I.

Car honking at another car this morning to stop for me.

Couple say happy birthday chalk and says "whos birthday is it?" I say I don't know but many people i've learned. She says "its his birthday today" I say well happy birthday. They walked back with the kids and daughter says "you get the happy birthday spot"

5/17/23
Boy on bike says yesterday two people made fun of his crocs but he ignored them. We talk about it, about how people can be mean and how they an have their own oppinions. We talked about how he felt and feels.

A little boy says he got sea monkeys- don't put puffer fish with them. He is teaching me so much about things I don't know about.

Cam asks will this be my assignment next year- I hope so I say. She says "even though its far from your house?" I tell her its one of the reasons I took the job was for some exercise. They've already tried to move me before.

5/18/23

While on my bike ride, I saw a boy from the high school was picking flowers along the path. He had a nice bouquet at this point.

As I was getting off my second shift, a guy driving by handed me a small water. I dislike that I had thoughts of bad intentions when he is such a sweet person. I then shift my thoughts to good people exist and had the thought what if I carry extra waters to pass out to people who may be in need.

I am going to miss a particular family who told me they are leaving. Which made me think of pen pals when I was younger. It may not be appropriate for me to be a pen pal but I will wonder about these kids and families as they leave and move to new places and live their lives.

Inspired, I write about pen pals. I wonder if this experience still exists.

"what, you were a teacher? Thank you we appreciate you" as they walk across

Little girl with dad and brother. Sister says hi it's my birthday today, dad's was other day. I hear them

having a discussion about what transparent means (based on translucent sea monkey writing)
Talked this morning with mom and two boys who loved sea monkey facts yesterday afternoon – I shared the facts I didn't write. Was it really national sea monkey day? She says. (that's what google said, what timing huh?)

5/19/23
"13 more days of this" "then it's summer break and you get a week off of this job to do whatever you want" says a little boy crossing.
I tell him well, I wont have this jobs but I will have other jobs. He asks if I have kids, I say yes four. His eyes open big in shock. His mom says "they want 4" laughing lol. "Well, now you have thousands of sea monkeys to deal with, so there's that lol

It's Friday and quite the day at work today.
*I have seen two grandparents walking kids who usually drive to school , this week. But this morning they say "It's been a pleasure seeing you , we probably wont see you after this because we are going back home today." It's been so nice seeing them.

*A mother walking with her stroller of two boys and daughter walking says "whats your name again? I know we asked before and heard people say it" I tell her and ask hers, I then learn the young girls name and I say "wow, my sister-in-law uses that name even though it isn't the one she was born with. beautiful name."

*so many pass the happy birthday drawing and say "who's birthday is it?" "is it your birthday?" I say no, it was someone from the houses over there but as days pass more and more share when it's there birthday . So it is for whomever it applies to. I then write under the drawing "is it your birthday? then this is for you"

*a young boy , his mom and brother were walking this morning and he is so excited saying things to me but I couldn't understand. He was wearing a mask and was a little distant but as he got closer and with the help of his mom I learned he was saying "our sea monkeys hatched today!" like a thousand of them. what are we going to do with them his mom says.
on the walk back, the younger brother runs to me with his hand open "look what I have" a ladybug

*this afternoon my daughters friend met me at work, to come with me to our house. While on our walk- so many things noticed that may not have been on a bike. like the crushed snails along the path.
or the crow and squirrel on the fence, the crow trying to get it. me yelling at luca to go scare the crow away. the crow coming back with friends.
while we passed the school we noticed a yard filled with adults and kids but in the corner were two boys, one very upset. So, I stop and ask "are you ok?" he says no. But the other boy quickly says "we are just joking around." I stay to ask more "are you good?" the boy not so open to speaking up anymore. But then the other kid give him back his phone. They are sharing words. It feels ok enough for me to walk away but I am

walking away upset that so many adults are present but not present.
and that luca, like me says "that kid was a bully"- if she notices and I do too. then maybe that was what it was.

5/22/23
A little boy says to the group he is walking with "this is a busy road." A mom says "that's why we have mrs lena" he says yea or else you could go splat.

Another mom says when her family walks not during school hours the boys always ask where I am. She says "she has a life"

5/23/23
Lean into the narrative or not.
A guy driving stops and says "what happened to the waving guy?" I say I am not sure. He says "you don't know" I say I don't, I have been here for a little over a year now, do you know his name? he says no but he would stand and wave to everybody all the time. Woman crossing says "was that person being nice?or weird? " I mention the waving guy and she says "he was nice, but that was a long time ago"

A woman walking who hasn't walked by much recently says "is your hair lighter? I am so not observant" I say yes and she says "was it like that this morning?" I say no, her son says its really nice hair. I say wow you are very observant.

A child with father driving, why is your hair down? I say because I went to the salon and I am trying to bring in the summer vibes. They say it looks amazing.

5/24/23
My daughters friend met me at work today. She did a drawing this afternoon. A car stops at the corner, a woman I have never seen before " do you do all of these chalk works?" she says no, I say I do. And she says "me an my kidslove them all around the neighborhood, I never knew who was doing them"

Two women walking, one I knew from my son's elementary school. She says lena? The other woman says "thank you for the chalk work, we love all of the affirmations and gratitides and jokes.

A dad walking with 3 kids is thinking out loud of certain foods that start with p....(in response to one of the questions)... Plantains!
I say thats a good one, I didn't think of that.

5/25/23
Stress: this job, them back in school, me not there to walk them or take them or see them dressed or check up. Them walking, the cars, fears. Not always someone to walk with.

5/26/23
(in response to the chalk scavenger hunt)
Girls with mom, wheres the house?

Two young boys "wheres the house will it be there tomorrow?"

Foods with "b" this time! Instead of P. Everyone was so excited the letter was changed and surprised.

5/29/23
A guy passing saw me drawing "I was wondering who does that. Its so awesome"

Memorial day, no school, no work.

5/30/23
Today I am not rushing to get home. I stayed after this morning, for morning chalk. On my bike by walgreens a guy says "are you a crossing guard? Me too, where at?"
A woman on bike waiting at the lights says "oh I live near there, are you the one that does all the chalk? I love seeing all of it all around. It's the little things. You really make peoples day, thank you"

Mom says "he's been going ahead of me pretending to be you" and says thank you.

$5 on ground biking. What gets you to stop fast in your tracks? What does it take for you to slow down. Is you gaining, someone else laching? Was it meant for you? Whats your sign?

5/31/23
What pieces of your work feel really important?

How do you let someone know how much you love
them
It cant be about the outcome

6/1/23
Guy drove by "did you color your hair?"

6/2/23
Highschooler "I like what you did with your hair.
Todays the last day of school, just finals now"

A mom stops to share with me.
Only been here 10months and leaving again. You are
our first happy cross guard. You make such a
difference. Even just getting us out our house door
knowing we will get to see you and the chalk and you
smiling. Going to r island then 1 more stop before
retirement. Everyone says it's like a dessert here but it
was so cold and wet these 10 months. So we didn't get
to do much. I know you more than our neighbors.

She is so right, it has been the coldest and most wet
winter ever, Not typical. Her comments to me and
about me really went straight to my heart. I apprceiate
the words, the time, the shares.

6/5/23
I always wonder who will move or stay. Sad but
exciting.
Create fun in the chaos. Find joy in the challenge. And
peace in the gratitude.

6/6/23

"we loved your note about moving" a mom says.

"so you will officially be unemployed?"
A man says as he is referring to summer coming up.
I say well yes for this job I will take a break, but- I still
have other things to do and jobs.

6/7/23

"whens your last day?" families are asking me.
Because the schools in this location get out on
different days and times.

Lady running "this is so cool, your messages"

Will you work summer school? A mom asks. But no,
we don't work summer. I think that is decided by the
school if it's needed but I am not sure.

Two boys on bikes. You get the "L" I ask what does "L
" stand for? Knowing but not wanting to assume. One
says loser and the other says liam. I say it can stand
for lena and I see no losers.
They stopped to share words about no one having to
be a loser. Then went about their way.

Lady walking dogs "have a great summer, I appreciate
you"
Guy walking dog reads jokes and laughs. Says out
loud "that's funny"
Car driving by , daddy got promoted- they screamed
from the car. I am so happy for their family.

Little boy in car doesn't go to school and says "ill miss you"

I had people who heard me, offered support, they became rescources, they had rescources. Answered prayers but different circumstances.

There's a Hawaiian family(they told me they are proud hawaiians) says they move this summer. "we appreciate and thank you" I barley saw them this year. "enjoy your next journey. Any plans this summer?" are you ready for it?

Mom with two boys, one in car. I ask if they are moving she says no then says well, you never know.

Are you ready for summer? Some will move, some will stay. I'll be here next year. Wishing you a beautiful summer. Reminder to pause sometimes. Time is not renewable rescource.

6/8/23
Last day of school
Mom this morning "we wont see you because we have 1 week of school left but thank you so much for making our days brighter. You really make a big difference. Thank you for being our crossing guard. Not all heros wear capes, some wear neon vests and chalk dust. " she said shes been trying to find a joke book to get me and shared how her son is getting into jokes now because of me.

Car drives by slowly and says "thank you for the work you do, I appreciate you.
Many asking if I will be back next year, here specifically.
A guy walking I have never seen ,"you keep our babies safe, thank you" peace and love
A dad who likes to share jokes walked over just to give me a card. And I had one for them. I walked to the school to hug and say bye. Mom says "we thrive in chaos, 9 straight day drive" to next destination.

Today as a summer gift, I passed out book marks this year. It's a slow day.

A boy where cross guard john is shared they exchange jokes. What a wonderful thing to learn.
You never know a different cross guards journey or experience.

Until next year, cheers to a break.
I will miss so many faces.
It will be sad not to see so many return.
And, I am grateful for all that has been shared in our time.

I wonder what it would be like to move around like people in the coast guard.

What lights you up about the work you do?

_____

_____

_____

_____

_____

_____

_____

_____

_____

How can you make your work more enjoyable?

_____

_____

_____

_____

_____

_____

_____

_____

_____

_____

What would it look like to walk in your purpose?

_____

_____

_____

_____

_____

_____

_____

_____

_____

_____

What do you naturally teach those around you?

_____

_____

_____

_____

_____

_____

_____

_____

_____

_____

_____

What is your dream job?

_____

_____

_____

_____

_____

_____

_____

_____

_____

_____

_____

What are your hobbies and passions? How does it differ from the work you do or the career you chose?

_____

_____

_____

_____

_____

_____

_____

_____

_____

What value have you given money? How do you allow
it to hold space in your life?

_____

_____

_____

_____

_____

_____

_____

_____

_____

What are you thankful for, right now?
(Challenge/invitation: something you can touch,
smell, taste, see, hear.)

_____

_____

_____

_____

_____

_____

_____

_____

_____

_____

What are you celebrating today? What have you accomplished?

_____

_____

_____

_____

_____

_____

_____

_____

_____

_____

Brain dump: let all your thoughts out. (don't overthink, just write.) For a whole minute...

_____

_____

_____

_____

_____

_____

_____

_____

_____

_____

If you had the day off, how would you love to spend it?

_____

_____

_____

_____

_____

_____

_____

_____

_____

_____

Do you see a weed or a wish? (dandelion) Is the cup
half full or half empty?

_____

_____

_____

_____

_____

_____

_____

_____

_____

_____

What would give your life more ease?

_____

_____

_____

_____

_____

_____

_____

_____

_____

_____

In what ways have you nourished yourself today? (mind, body, spirit)

_____

_____

_____

_____

_____

_____

_____

_____

_____

_____

_____

What serves you, when you are feeling overwhelmed?

_____

_____

_____

_____

_____

_____

_____

_____

_____

_____

About the Author

Cross guard Chronicles, the diary continues is author Carolina's 7th self-published book (6th for distribution.) Carolina, also known as Lena has taken a break from being a teacher and embraced other passions and purposes. One of those callings, being an author, sharing gratitude and inviting others to partake in journaling and reflecting. She loves being a wife, mother, daughter, sister, friend, family member, coach and homeschool mama.

A note to my readers

I hope if you take anything away that you allow your curiosity to lead. Ask questions, dig deeper, and give yourself permission to be. Allow fun whenever you can and know that learning (and teaching) is all around us, all the time. However, you ended up with this book, I am thankful for you being here and I celebrate you for who you are in this world and what you mean to my journey.

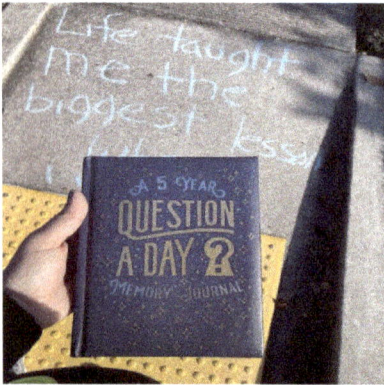

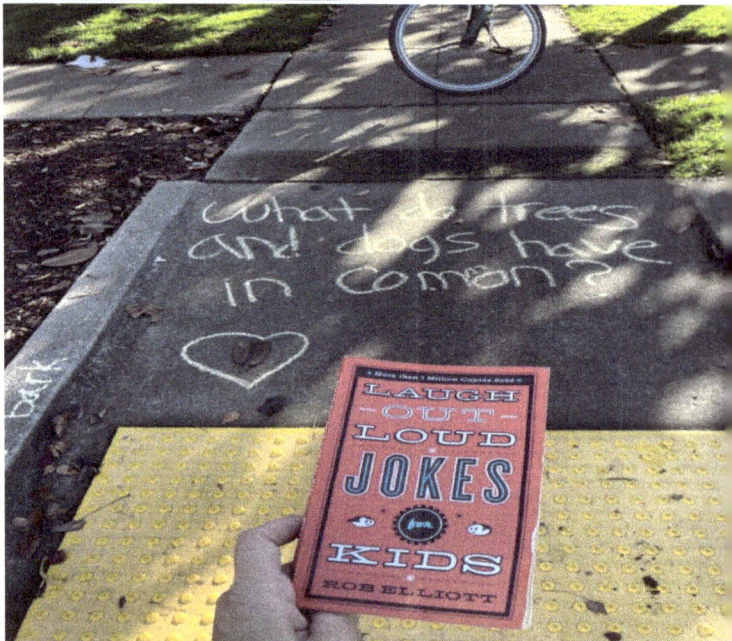

Can you find any of these on your walk?

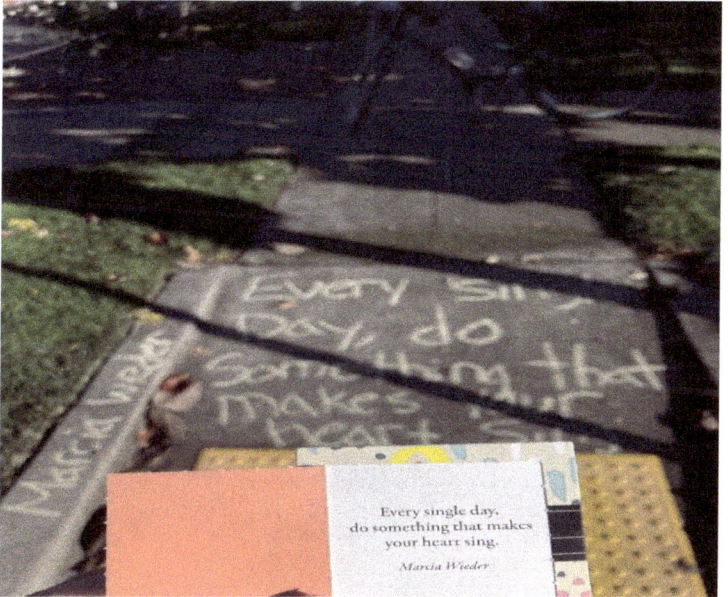

Marcia Wieder

Every single day,
do something that makes
your heart sing.

Marcia Wieder

HOW ARE YOU?

Check it with
yourself as
much as you
need to

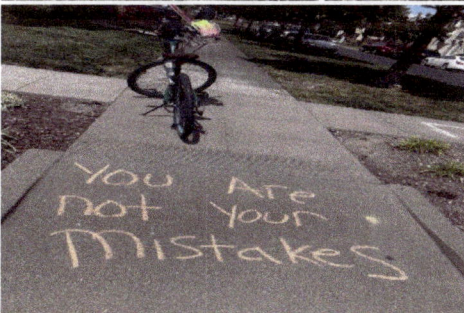

You Are not your Mistakes

121

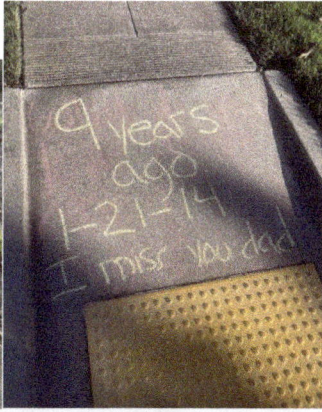

9 years
ago
1-21-14
I miss you dad

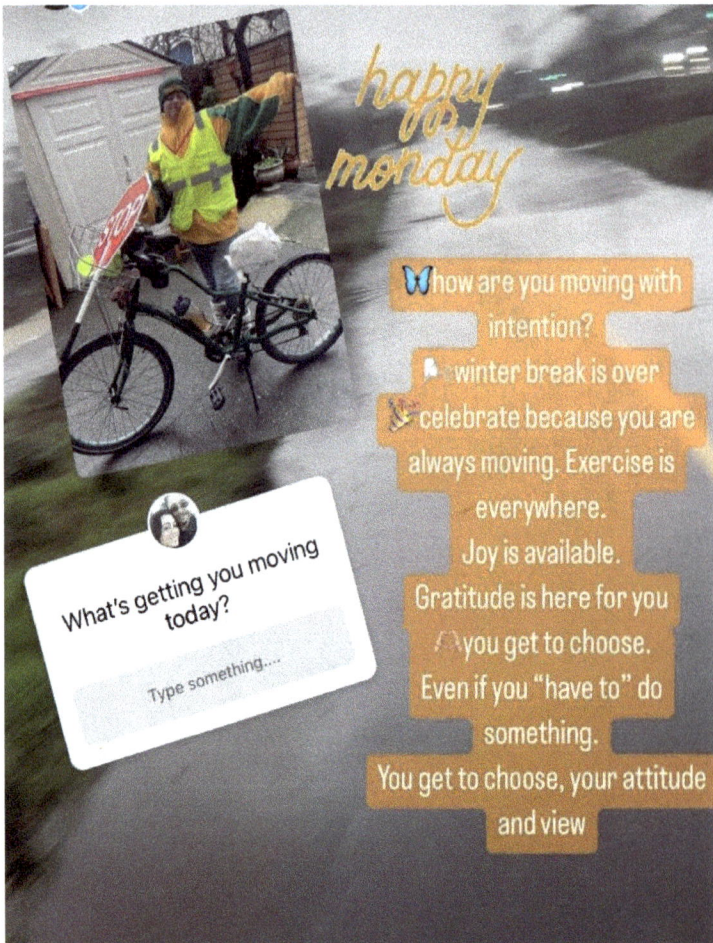

how are you moving with intention?
winter break is over
celebrate because you are always moving. Exercise is everywhere.
Joy is available.
Gratitude is here for you
you get to choose.
Even if you "have to" do something.
You get to choose, your attitude and view

happy monday

What's getting you moving today?

Type something....

Part 3 will be coming in 2024, until next time... make time for the things that fill you with joy.